TIPS

Establishing a String and Orchestra Program

Compiled by
Jacquelyn Dillon-Krass
and Dorothy A. Straub

MENC

The National Association for Music Education

Table of Contents

Foreword

The Music Educators National Conference (MENC) has created the TIPS series to provide music educators with a variety of ideas on a wide range of practical subjects. Each *TIPS* booklet is a compilation of methods, ideas, and suggestions that have been successful in the music classroom. MENC has designed this quick-reference series to be used as a starting point for creating and adapting projects for your particular situation. *TIPS: Establishing a String and Orchestra Program* is designed for the music teacher, music administrator, general adminis-trator, parent, or community member interested in initiating a success-ful string and orchestra program in a school district.

Rationale

Why Have a String Program?

No school music program can be considered complete unless it includes an orchestra program. A vast cultural heritage of artistic achievement in music lies within the orchestral genre. To ignore it is to overlook an area of one's humanistic, artistic, and intellectual education. All children should be provided with opportunities to pursue their interests and talents. Any school professing to offer a balanced instrumental program must offer instruction on all traditional instruments, including strings.

Every school system should offer stringed instrument instruction at all levels because:

- According to the Music Educators National Conference publication *The School Music Program: Description and Standards*, the musical life of any school cannot be considered good or even basic quality without an orchestra.
- Every student is entitled to the opportunity to explore classroom activities, vocal activities, and the study of a band or orchestra instrument during his or her public school career.
- For many individuals, the study of a stringed instrument provides the most direct means of integrating hands, head, and heart—furthering physical, intellectual, and expressive growth. Contrary to popular misconceptions, stringed instruments are easily taught. A beginning group can sound good and can play tunes parents can recognize after just a few lessons.
- A school music program without orchestral activities seriously shortchanges those individuals who wish to study a stringed instrument and denies woodwind, brass, percussion, and vocal students the experience of performing with an orchestra. Orchestral experience for wind and percussion players provides solo responsibilities not common in a typical band program and develops increased musicianship. Without strings, the great masterworks for chorus and orchestra cannot be performed as originally written. Denial of the opportunity to perform orchestral music hampers full musical development of any musician.
- The orchestra's literature is one of Western culture's greatest treasures. Symphonic music is heard and enjoyed on radio, television, and in films, as well as in the concert hall. A school orches-

1

tra is valuable not only for its participants, but for the school and community.

- Many students are attracted to the sound of stringed instruments or to the music written for strings. If a child prefers the sound of an orchestra to that of a band, he or she should be given the option of participating in an orchestra program. If a string program is not offered, these students probably will not become involved in music.
- Many colleges and universities seek string players for their orchestras. Scholarships may be available to competent string players.
- Community orchestras welcome capable string players at a high school level and above. Music productions and performances of joint choral and orchestral works are popular in communities that support orchestra programs. Lifelong opportunities for playing stringed instruments abound: according to the American Symphony Orchestra League, adults in this country have access to 1,650 orchestras as well as countless smaller groups such as quartets or trios.

There are many reasons for the absence of school orchestras. Successful string and orchestra programs, however, thrive in school districts where a commitment has been made to their success. Programs have been successfully initiated (with impressive results) throughout the country under a variety of demographic and socioeconomic circumstances. The key ingredient seems to be administrative willingness to make a commitment to the program's success, combined with an appropriate schedule, adequate funds, and properly trained and enthusiastic teachers.

* * *

Goals of the String Program

First-Year Goals

The goal of the program is to create a balanced school orchestra in each elementary school and to maintain a high percentage of beginning students, who, at end of the year, enroll in the second-year program.

Instructional goals:

You should refer to MENC's *Teaching Stringed Instruments: A Course of Study* for a detailed explanation of instructional goals for the first level. Generally though, by the end of the first year, students should be able to:

- Play with a good holding position and correct left- and right-hand positions.
- Play with a steady beat.
- Play with accurate intonation.
- Read notes and understand first position notes in the key of D major and possibly in G major.
- Play music with time signatures of $\frac{4}{4}$, $\frac{3}{4}$, and possibly $\frac{2}{4}$.
- Play music that makes use of quarter notes, half notes, whole notes, and corresponding rests.
- Play music with slurs and ties.
- Play some familiar unison melodies, and possibly one or two simple harmonized orchestrations.
- Cover most of Book One of a string method.

Performance goals:

Include a demonstration program for parents sometime during the first year in each school; a late spring concert of string students combined from all elementary schools that offer a string program; and a concert for potential beginners, including an informal presentation about how they can begin during the next year.

Promotional goals:

The goal here is to ensure that the community is well aware that the school system has a new string and orchestra program. Some suggestions:

- During the recruiting period, submit a picture and an article to your local newspaper to provide information about the new program. You should also try to submit photographs and articles to your local newspaper before the combined concert. (Pictures of rehearsals attract more interest than long articles.) All communications and publicity materials should be approved by the administration (principal or superintendent) prior to publication.

- Help parents form an organization to assist with some of the non-teaching aspects of the program. Members of such an organization could serve as a telephone committee, do public relations work for the string program, serve as chaperones for field trips, or take on fund-raising tasks if necessary.

* * *

Long-Range Goals

Long-range goals of your program should include:

- Providing for continuous, sequential instruction at each grade level—including development on individual instruments and orchestral literature.
- Developing the orchestra program as an integral component of the music program.
- Implementing string classes and orchestra in every elementary school.
- Implementing an orchestra program in the middle/junior high schools. This program should consist of both a string orchestra and a full orchestra with woodwinds, brass, and percussion. Cooperation with the school band director is important.
- Implementing an orchestra program in the high school. The senior high program should offer a full orchestra, place greater emphasis on performance, and enable students to participate in regional and all-state activities.
- Projecting string enrollment for each level—elementary, middle school/junior high, high school.
- Planning schedules for middle school/junior high and high school programs. At least two or three classes should be offered per week.
- Preparing a budget and projecting needs for additional staff, additional instruments, full-sized cellos and basses for secondary schools, the purchase of orchestra music, and compilation of an orchestra music library.
- Developing a written curriculum for the string and orchestra program from the beginning level through the high school level. (Refer to *Teaching Stringed Instruments: A Course of Study*.)

* * *

Where to Find Help

People and Organizations

Many people and organizations will help interested educators establish an orchestra program. Do not be afraid to seek assistance. Some suggestions:

- Call your state music or fine arts consultant and ask him or her to identify school districts similar to yours in size and economics where successful string programs exist. Consultants should be able to give you names of people responsible for such programs.
- Visit a successful school orchestra program. An experienced, successful string and orchestra teacher may be your most valuable source of information and support.
- Contact the president of state music education association for the names of state or regional leaders of the American String Teachers Association (ASTA) and the National School Orchestra Association (NSOA). These organizations now have hot lines you may call for assistance. The ASTA hot line number is 404-262-ASTA. For the NSOA hot line number, see *The Bulletin* of NSOA. For information on NSOA call MENC's membership department at 703-860-4000. The state president may also be able to recommend helpful Suzuki teachers or programs.
- Contact string education instructors at state universities. They are usually knowledgeable about school string programs.
- Don't forget to draw on other school and community resources. Other people who could help plan the program or offer support include: music administrators and teachers in the school district, youth symphony conductors and officers, local retail music dealers, stringed instrument distributors or manufacturers, amateur and professional musicians in the community, private stringed-instrument teachers, symphony orchestra supporters, community arts organizations, and interested parents.

* * *

Information in Print

You can gather helpful information from the following sources:

- MENC publications such as *The School Music Program: Description and Standards*, 1986; *The Complete String Guide: Standards,*

5

Programs, Purchase, and Maintenance, 1988; *Teaching Stringed Instruments: A Course of Study*, 1991; and related articles from *Music Educators Journal* .

- Selected articles from *American String Teacher*, published quarterly by the American String Teachers Association (see the Selected Readings).
- Selected articles from *The Instrumentalist* (see the Selected Readings).
- *The Bulletin*, the quarterly magazine for members of the National School Orchestra Association.
- Promotional materials, available on request from stringed instrument companies, that provide information on topics such as recruitment, choosing an instrument, parental support, teaching aids, and other related topics.
- Books on the subject (see the Selected Readings).

* * *

Seeking Administrative Approval

Influencing Decision Makers

Before meeting with any administrator or administrative body, the program must have the interest of the community and the concerted support of the music faculty. You may need to plant the seeds of community interest. Parents of prospective students and informed, influential people can lend support to the proposed program.

If you meet with your school superintendent or another appropriate administrator, be prepared to give a rationale for a string program. You should also come prepared with a tentative plan for the program's first year, including information on scheduling, staffing, equipment, and budget. Offer to assist the administrator with communication to principals, music faculty, parents, and the community.

If you present a proposal to a board of education, the proposal should also include a plan for the program's first year. If funds are limited, consider a pilot program in one or two schools. On successful completion of the pilot, you will need to project a long-range plan of three to five years. Presenting models of successful programs in your area may be helpful.

* * *

Scheduling

In determining a schedule, choose one that best suits your school system. A variety of successful patterns exist. You will need to make three critical decisions in scheduling your orchestra program.

1. *In what grade should the program begin?* Most programs begin in grade four or five. Some programs begin as early as grade three, while others begin in grade six. There are successful programs that begin one year before the band program, as well as some that begin in the same grade.

2. *How often should classes meet?* Most successful programs schedule beginners for at least two meetings per week. As a minimum requirement, string classes should meet at least as frequently as the band program.

   Before making these first two decisions, consider these facts:

   - Stringed instruments are available in small sizes, making it possible for young children to begin on stringed instruments.
   - Playing a stringed instrument necessitates adequate instructional time for establishing good habits in the beginning stages.
   - Orchestra programs that allow students to enroll a year before they are eligible for the band program facilitate the recruiting of string players and give string players a head start on the challenging stringed instruments. Programs that begin the same year as the band program decrease the likelihood that students will drop out of the orchestra to join the band program and decrease competition between band and orchestra.
   - If seventh-grade students are expected to perform in an orchestra at an intermediate level, instruction should begin two or three years prior to grade seven. The organizational structure of your school system (the grouping of grade levels) will be a major concern as you plan what ensembles you will offer at each level.

3. *When should instruction take place?* In most successful programs, orchestra students receive instruction during the regular school day. There are many possible schedules that can be used. At the elementary level, you can use a rotating schedule that allows students to be taken from other subjects only once in several weeks. Consider a schedule that follows the schedul-

ing pattern of the band program. A schedule that allows for band and orchestra to meet at the same time minimizes interruptions for the classroom teacher.

At the middle school or junior high and high school levels, most successful programs meet as regularly scheduled classes at least two or three times each week. Instruction at this level should include technical development on an individual instrument (a rotating lesson schedule may be used) and orchestral experience within a large ensemble that performs orchestral literature.

* * *

Staffing

Who Will Teach the Classes?

A successful pilot course taught by existing staff in one or more schools can provide tangible evidence of interest for a systemwide string program. A band teacher or classroom music specialist with a string background or interest in a string program may be able to add a class of beginning strings. (Teaching schedules may need to be altered.)

Using existing staff, however, is a temporary measure for starting a program. Following the first year, students will need instruction at a second-year level and new beginners will need to start in a separate class. Therefore, more teaching time will be needed for strings. The presence of a qualified string teacher also becomes more critical in the second year.

Once the school administration is assured that there will be enough student participation in the string program, you can more easily defend a request for new staff. Justification for hiring new staff members is easier to obtain if some students have been recruited, have begun to play, and need continued instruction.

* * *

When hiring a teacher for the beginning orchestra program, look for:
- A good teacher and good musician. (This is first and foremost.)
- Pedagogical knowledge of all stringed instruments.
- Playing proficiency on at least one stringed instrument.
- Commitment to the development of a string program.

When making staff decisions, consider the makeup of the classes. Are classes homogeneous (all violins, for example) or heterogeneous (all stringed instruments together)? Are large groups or small groups being taught in the classes?

The "right" person is key to the success of the program. Look for someone who is well organized, enthusiastic, cooperative, creative, and task oriented, who is a good communicator, and who displays leadership ability and a positive attitude. Successful experience as a string educator is highly desirable.

* * *

To find a qualified teacher:
- Contact universities with a string teacher training program.
- Consult private or university placement services.

- Inform key people of your need for a teacher. Good contacts include music or arts administrators in your state department of education, state music educators association leaders, state or regional leaders of American String Teachers Association or National School Orchestra Association, and successful string educators or music administrators in other districts.

* * *

To determine how much staff time is needed to begin the program, consider:
- The number of schools that will offer a program. (Remember that schedules should allow time before and after classes for arranging instructional space and equipment, as well as time for travel from school to school.)
- The grade level (or levels) at which beginners will start.
- The number of students who will participate from each school.
- The number of classes that will be offered and how much time will be allotted per class. (A minimum of two thirty-minute classes per week is needed for each group.)

* * *

Plans for Program Expansion

In the second year, your staff will be responsible for teaching both continuing students and new beginners and implementing the orchestra program in additional schools. In the third year and beyond, your staff will need to teach first-, second-, and third-year students. The staff will also be responsible for planning and implementing orchestra programs at the middle school/junior high school and high school levels, so expansion of the program into the secondary level will require more staff. Qualified string specialists are particularly desirable at this level.

* * *

Professional Development of the String Teacher

If you start a program with existing staff, make provisions for training teachers in the basic fundamentals of string-class teaching. School administrators should allocate funds for in-service training for string teachers *before* implementation of the program and during the program's early development. A successful school orchestra director in another district may be able to help you in planning this aspect of your program.

Participation in workshops, clinics, and conferences is necessary for both new and experienced teachers to stay current with pedagogy,

11

teaching techniques, and orchestral literature. The professional journals of The Music Educators National Conference (MENC), The American String Teachers Association (ASTA), and The National School Orchestra Association (NSOA) usually list such events. Also, many universities offer summer clinics in string teaching.

* * *

Facilities, Equipment, and Supplies

For proper instruction, each school needs the following:

- A quiet rehearsal room, acoustically separate from other classrooms and away from noise. It should be large enough to accommodate small-group lessons or large-ensemble rehearsals. Adequate open space is needed, preferably with a flat floor (no risers). If facilities are limited, a separate place for large-group rehearsal may be necessary. A band room, for example, could be shared with the string program, with cooperative scheduling.
- Standard-size chairs with flat seats and no arms.
- Enough music stands for a large-group rehearsal.
- A tuning device.
- Access to a piano.
- A chalkboard.
- Funds to purchase music for the orchestra.
- Access to a stereo system and/or cassette playback.

Each school needs proper storage space for instruments that children bring to school. The space must be safe and secure to avoid instrument damage or theft. It should be neither excessively hot nor cold and should have both shelves (for violins and violas) and racks or closet space (for cellos and basses).

* * *

Obtaining Instruments

It is preferable for parents to provide an instrument for their children (violins and violas, perhaps cellos, if available). This fosters commitment to the instrument and program. Learn about the economic resources of your community to determine if asking parents to bear the responsibility for acquiring an instrument is feasible.

Investigate the instrument rental programs in your area. Most retail music dealers have rental programs for stringed instruments. Obtain a copy of their rental agreements and seek specific information from each dealer, such as:

- Does the dealer offer all stringed instruments?
- Is the rental period limited (three to nine months) or unlimited?
- Does the dealer provide for changing sizes ($\frac{1}{2}$ to $\frac{3}{4}$ and $\frac{3}{4}$ to $\frac{4}{4}$ size)?
- Do rental fees apply toward the purchase of an instrument?
- Does the dealer rent new or used instruments?
- What is the quality and condition of the instruments?
- Are the rental and purchase prices reasonable and competitive?
- Does the dealer provide for repair of instruments rented and purchased?
- What other services are offered? (These services may include pickup and delivery to school, loaner instruments, free folders, and cooperation in offering clinics and in-service sessions.)

* * *

School-Owned Instruments

In communities where it is not possible for parents to provide instruments for their children, the school district needs to acquire an inventory of all the stringed instruments: violins, violas, cellos, and basses. Many school systems issue school-owned instruments for a nominal rental fee.

If local dealers do not have a rental program for cellos and basses, the school district needs to purchase or lease these instruments. A plan for purchase of school-owned stringed instruments needs to be developed.

Devise a plan for the first year. For example, a K–5 elementary school would need two to six cellos and two to four basses in the first year.

To devise a five-year instrument purchase plan, project the number of cellos and basses needed per grade per school. Secure help from an experienced person to prepare the projections. Plan to purchase the correct sizes of instruments, appropriate for each grade level.

School districts can obtain instruments in two ways:

1. *Purchasing through the school bid process.* Be sure to get advice from a person experienced in writing school stringed-instrument bids. Details on materials, workmanship, quality, shop-adjustment, delivery, and replacement policy must all be clearly stated on the bid.
2. *A lease program from national stringed instrument companies.* Leases usually involve three- to five-year plans.

You may wish to evaluate a sample of an unknown brand or model of an instrument. Most dealers are willing to help with this.

* * *

Sizes of Stringed Instruments

- Violin—½ , ¾ , and 4/4 sizes are available. (Smaller violins and cellos—¼ to ⅛ size—are available for small students.) Fourth graders will generally need ½ and ¾ sizes, fifth graders will need mostly ¾ size instruments. Sixth graders will need ¾ and 4/4 sizes, with seventh graders usually needing 4/4 size.
- Viola—junior (thirteen-inch), intermediate (fourteen-inch), and full sizes are available. Full-size violas vary from fifteen to seventeen inches. Fourth graders will generally need junior size violas, with fifth graders needing junior and intermediate sizes. Intermediate-size violas are appropriate for sixth graders. Seventh graders will need fifteen-inch violas.
- Cello—½, ¾, and 4/4 sizes are available. Fourth graders will generally need ½ and ¾ sizes. Fifth graders will need mostly ¾ size instruments, with sixth graders needing ¾ and 4/4 sizes. Most seventh graders are ready for 4/4 size cellos.
- String bass—¼ (junior), ½, and ¾ sizes are available (¾ bass is the standard adult-size bass). Fourth graders will need ¼ size basses, with fifth graders needing ¼ and ½ sizes. Sixth graders will need ¼ and ½ sizes. Seventh graders will need ½ size basses. Both ½ and ¾ sizes will be needed by eighth graders, and ninth graders will need ¾ size basses. Measurements of small basses are inconsistent from one company to another. There is no true ¼ size bass. Students must be furnished with appropriately sized instruments if they are to play comfortably and learn successfully.
- Due to a scarcity of cellos and basses manufactured worldwide, there is often a delay in delivery. Allow additional time for delivery.

- A "measuring stick" specifically designed for stringed instrument sizing is available from stringed instrument companies. In measuring students and assigning instruments, keep in mind that it is better for a student to play an instrument that is too small than one that is too large.

* * *

Recruitment of Students

The purpose of a recruiting process is to acquaint students with the instruments that will be taught, to guide students in choosing the appropriate instrument, and to inform students about string classes and the program. During recruitment, students should receive information about how to enroll in the string program.

Note: If music aptitude tests are given, results should be used to encourage rather than exclude participation in the program.

* * *

Teacher Attitude and Underlying Philosophy

The personality and enthusiasm of the teacher is the most important factor in influencing a student to play an instrument. Do present the personality that is uniquely yours: don't try to duplicate another teacher's style.

Children respond positively to a teacher who is sincere and reflects a genuine love of children. Positive teacher attitude is vital to successful results in recruiting. Assume the attitude that every child wants to play; your role is to assist them in choosing an instrument.

* * *

Preparation for Recruitment

Set up a demonstration schedule for students who are eligible to begin learning a stringed instrument. Be sure to work with general music teachers and to get approval from the school administration before approaching classroom teachers. Consider these suggestions:

- A presentation to a small group is usually most effective. Present short (twenty- to thirty-minute) demonstrations in individual classrooms rather than in a school assembly.
- Try to include good student musicians who already play. Each instrument that will be taught should be demonstrated.
- Place special emphasis on the larger instruments (viola, cello, and bass) so that student interest will not be limited to the violin.
- If possible, give your stringed-instrument presentation separately from the band-instrument presentation, preferably after.
- Arrange for an evening parents' meeting. You will need to reserve space in your school, plan the setup, speak to your school

custodian, and arrange for assistance from other music teachers and older students.

* * *

Communication with Music Dealers

Inform local dealers of the recruitment dates and dates for starting the program. Provide dealers with a copy of printed materials about enrollment in the string program given to students and parents. Tell local music dealers what method book you will use and ask them to ascertain its availability.

Ask to use some of the music dealers' instruments in the demonstration. Ask dealers if they have pertinent promotional materials; request these materials well in advance of the recruitment period so that they will be available when you need them.

Dealers may offer helpful suggestions about recruiting. Some dealers may even assist with the recruiting demonstrations and provide printed materials about their rental program. If the school district permits, you may wish to invite local dealers to participate in an evening parents' meeting for prospective students. This may be done in conjunction with the beginning band parents' night.

* * *

Recruitment Letter or Brochure

Write and distribute a letter or brochure to all students in the eligible grade level and to their parents. In the letter:

- State the value of the program for the child.
- State your school district's commitment to its new string program. Explain that developing a high school orchestra is the goal.
- Outline opportunities for string players in school and as adults, including: college scholarships, participation in community orchestras, and performance of all types of music from classical to popular.
- Describe the program—what instruments will be taught, when groups will meet, and when classes are to begin.
- Explain that there is no charge for instruction because the program is part of your school's regular music program.
- Outline performance goals for the year.
- Explain how to enroll, and include an enrollment form to be returned with pertinent information such as: child's name, grade, and homeroom teacher; parent's name, address, and phone; and choice of instrument. (It is best to ask students to list their first and second choice instruments.)

- Explain how to obtain an instrument and recommend that students rent or lease at first.
- Give the date, time, place, and purpose of the evening parents' meeting and explain how to get additional information.
- Emphasize the importance of parental involvement from the start.

* * *

The Demonstration for Students

Give each child a letter or brochure to take home to parents. Remind children to take the information home, tell their parents what instrument they would like to study, and return the registration form. Also remind students of the importance of attending the evening meeting with their parents.

Your presentation should be short, fast paced, and fun. Show and play all four stringed instruments. Include student string players in the presentation, if possible; peer influence is a positive and effective recruiting tool.

You may also ask other appropriate string players to perform. They may include players from local music stores, student musicians from outside your school district, youth symphony members, college students, or private teachers.

Musical selections performed should include solo pieces for each instrument, to demonstrate characteristic sounds. Other pieces should demonstrate a full ensemble (two violins, viola, cello, and bass if possible.) Perform tunes the children will enjoy or recognize, such as fiddle tunes, folk music, themes from masterworks, popular melodies, or themes from television commercials and programs. Include a brief, full-sounding example from the string ensemble literature (such as Bach's *Brandenburg Concerto* no. 3, Haydn's "Surprise" Symphony, or Mozart's *Eine kleine Nachtmusik*).

Be sure that the demonstration is not centered around the violin. Build in extra encouragement for viola, cello, and especially bass. If the stringed instrument presentation is part of a total instrumental music presentation, be sure to include extra motivation for prospective string players.

On the reverse side of the letter to parents, ask each student to draw an outline of his or her left hand. Explain the characteristics of hands best suited for each stringed instrument. A narrow hand with long fingers is generally good for violin and viola. A broad hand with short fingers is generally better suited for cello and bass (see figure 1). Ask each child to write the name of the instrument best suited for his or her hand.

Violin Hand
Medium-sized hand—equal spacing between the first and second, and third fingers.

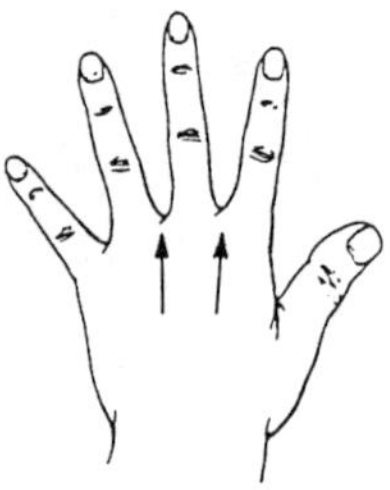

Cello Hand
Large, sturdy hand with wide spaces between all fingers so they can "stretch" easily.

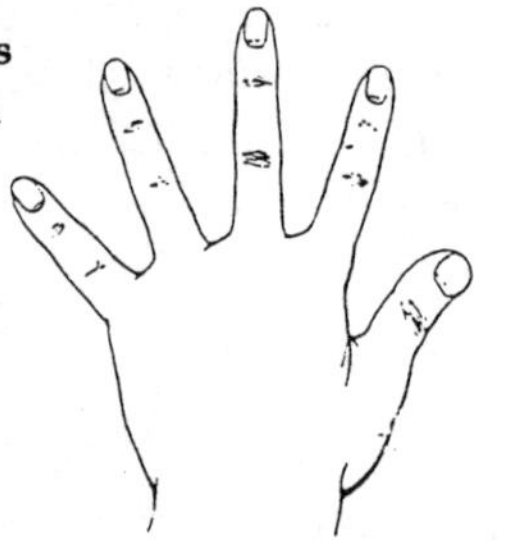

Viola Hand
Longer and thinner than the Violin Hand, with longer fingers; especially the "pinkie" (fourth finger). Equal spacing between first and second, and second and third fingers.

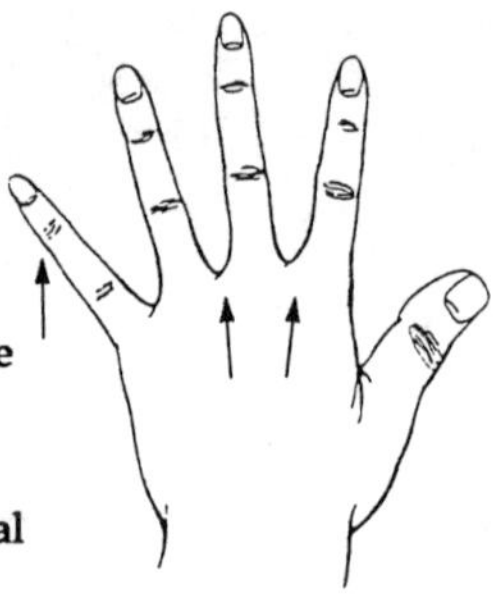

Bass Hand
Large, strong, stocky hand with spacing between the first and second fingers equal to the space between the second and fourth fingers.

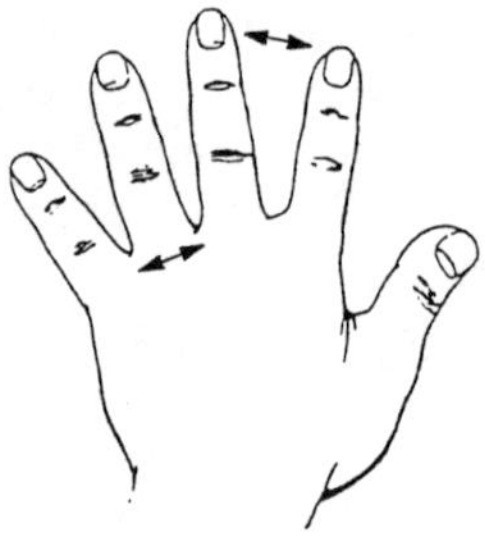

Figure 1. Hand chart for string players.
Reprinted from the Fall 1978 issue of *Orchestra News*. Used with permission of the editor.

Determine the proportion of students enrolled for each instrument that you will need to create a balanced orchestra in each school. For example, with twenty-four beginning string students, twelve could play violin, six play viola, four play cello, and two play bass.

* * *

Follow-Up

As registration forms are returned:

- Influence students to choose instruments that will balance the enrollment.
- Talk with your school's vocal and general music teachers and seek their continued support. Ask these music teachers to identify talented students who should be included in the string program and to provide information about individual students and their potential.
- Talk with classroom teachers, asking them to identify leaders and provide additional helpful information about students.
- Call parents of students who are not enrolled but who have been recommended by music or classroom teachers.
- Use students already enrolled to encourage their friends to join.
- Place reminders about program enrollment in school announcements and newsletters. Attractive posters throughout the school can be effective.
- Ask classroom teachers to remind students to return their enrollment forms.
- Place a notice about the program in the local newspaper. You might include a photograph from the recruiting session.

* * *

Conclusion

The ideas in this *TIPS* booklet are meant to be helpful to those sincerely interested in adding a string and orchestra component to their school music program. The focus is on establishing programs that will be successful, and therefore will be continued and maintained.

The challenge may seem overwhelming, but the adventure is well worth the effort when you measure the yield in terms of musical experiences for children.

You will be pleased to find generous willingness to help you at each step of the way.

Enjoy sharing the rewards with fortunate young musicians. Good luck!

Selected Readings

Chusmir, Marsha. "Teaching Strings: A Special Opportunity for Wind and Percussion Majors." *American String Teacher* 24, no. 3 (1974): 6.

The Complete String Guide. Reston, VA: Music Educators National Conference, 1988.

Culver, Robert. "Goals of a String Program." *American String Teacher* 31, no. 3 (1981): 21–24.

Culver, Robert. "Survivors: Quality School Orchestra Programs." *American String Teacher* 34, no. 2 (1984): 42–43.

Dillon, Jacquelyn A. "Building and Maintaining Your String Program: Getting the Students You Need." *Music Performance Resource* (Spring 1988).

Dillon, Jacquelyn A. "How to Educate Parents for a Better String Program." In *Voices of Industry*. Reston, VA: Music Educators National Conference, 1990.

Dillon, Jacquelyn A. "Schools Should Orchestrate Orchestras." In *Conn Chord*. Elkhart, IN: C.G. Conn Ltd., 1978.

Dillon, Jacquelyn A. "Twenty Tips for Successful String Class Recruiting." *Orchestra News* 17, no. 1 (Spring 1979).

Dillon, Jacquelyn A. "What is Your Recruiting Quotient?" *American String Teacher* 30, no. 2 (1980): 24.

Dillon, Jacquelyn A., and Casimer Kriechbaum. *How to Design and Teach a Successful School String and Orchestra Program*. San Diego, CA: Kjos West, 1978.

Edwards, Arthur C. *Beginning String Class Method*. Dubuque, IA: William C. Brown, 1985.

Englehardt, D. "Successful Beginning String Programs." *The Instrumentalist* 31 (September 1979): 36–37.

Evans, Judith. "The Importance of a Good Instrument to the Success of the Beginner." *Orchestra News* 17, no. 1 (Spring 1979).

Green, Elizabeth A.H. *Teaching String Instruments In Classes*. Englewood Cliffs, NJ: Prentice Hall, 1966. (Distributed by Theodore Presser.)

Henkle, Ted. "To the Band Director." *American String Teacher* 21, no. 4 (1971): 6.

Iams, C. Gary. "Recruiting Strings." *The Instrumentalist*. Reprinted in *The Best of Soundpost*. Pittsburgh, PA: National School Orchestra Association, 1976.

Kjelland, James. "String-o-phobia: Some Causes and Cures." *American String Teacher* 37, no. 2 (1987): 70–74.

Kriechbaum, Casimer, and Kay Kirtley. "How to Recruit String Students for a String Program." *Orchestra News* 16, no. 2 (Fall 1978).

Lamb, Norman. *Guide to Teaching Strings*. 4th ed. Dubuque, IA: William C. Brown, 1984.

Matesky, Ralph. *Playing and Teaching Stringed Instruments*. 2 vols. Englewood Cliffs, NJ: Prentice Hall, 1963.

Miller, D. "Initiating an Elementary String Program." *The Instrumentalist* 22 (November 1967): 44–45.

Oddo, Vincent. *Playing and Teaching the Strings*. Belmont, CA: Wadsworth Publishing Inc., 1979.

Rohr, J. "Organizing an Elementary String Program." *The Instrumentalist* 21 (February 1967): 48.

The School Music Program: Description and Standards. Reston, VA: Music Educators National Conference, 1986.

Scott, S. "The Converted Band Director." *American String Teacher* 17, no.1 (1967): 48.

Shaw, G. Jean. "Why Not Add Strings to Your Music Program?" *The School Musician* 40 (April 1969): 66–67.

Stycos, R. *School Orchestra Director's Guide.* Portland, ME: J. Weston Walch, 1982.

Stevens, A. "Recruiting the Strings." *The Instrumentalist* 21 (November 1966): 43–45.

Teaching Stringed Instruments: A Course of Study. Reston, VA: Music Educators National Conference, 1991.

Witt, Anne C. *Recruiting for the School Orchestra.* Elkhart, IN: The Selmer Company, 1984.

Acknowledgments

The material in this *TIPS* booklet is the product of a series of meetings of the MENC Ad Hoc Committee on String and Orchestra Education. Committee members include:

Robert Culver—American String Teachers Association; Professor of Music Education—University of Michigan, Ann Arbor, Michigan

Sandra Dackow—National School Orchestra Association; Conductor—Brandeis University Boston, Massachusetts

Jacquelyn Dillon-Krass—Music Industry Conference; Educational Director—Scherl & Roth, a subsidiary of Conn Ltd.; Professor of String Education—Friends University Wichita, Kansas

Gerald Doan—American String Teachers Association; Director of String Education—University of Cincinnati Cincinnati, Ohio

Robert Johnson—Music Industry Conference; Glaesel (Selmer Company), Elkhart, Indiana

Jerry Kupchynsky—National School Orchestra Association; Music Coordinator—East Brunswick, New Jersey

Paul Landefeld—Suzuki Association of the Americas; Director—Suzuki School Muscatine, Iowa

Harriet Mogge—Music Educators National Conference; Director of Meetings and Conventions—MENC, Reston, Virginia

Robert Reinsager—Suzuki Association of the Americas; Executive Director Muscatine, Iowa

Dorothy A. Straub—Music Educators National Conference; Music Coordinator—Fairfield Public Schools, Fairfield, Connecticut

Pamela Tellejohn—National School Orchestra Association; Coordinator of Orchestra Program—Richland District 2, Columbia, South Carolina

25